**THAT'S LIFE
PictureStories**

BOOK 4
In a Family Way

Tana Reiff

LAKE EDUCATION
Belmont, California

The Marcianos

■ Frank Marciano *He owns a grocery store and has something to say on every subject.*

■ Marge Marciano *She listens to everyone's problems and knows how to help.*

■ Ernesto Marciano *Frank's father retires from life until he meets Rosa Esteban.*

■ Gina Marciano *The Marcianos' daughter is very much her own woman.*

■ Doug Kelly *He and Gina Marciano have a life plan that works for them.*

The Adamses

■ Walter Adams *Keeping up with a growing family has its problems.*

■ Ruth Adams *She manages to keep her cool through all of life's surprises.*

■ Pat Adams *A 13-year-old learns something new about life every day.*

■ Tyrone Adams *At 16, does "Mr. Basketball" really know it all?*

The Estebans

■ Carlos Esteban *Since his wife's death, he's both father and mother to his children.*

■ Rosa Esteban *Carlos's mother doesn't let age stand in the way of happiness.*

■ Rick Esteban *He finds that it's easy to get in trouble when you're 16.*

■ Roberto Esteban *This 14-year-old boy is making big plans for his future.*

■ Bonita Esteban *Growing up means having to learn about all sides of life.*

The Nguyens

■ Nguyen Lan *She can handle being a single parent in a new country.*

■ Nguyen Tam *At 4, he asks his mother why he has no father at home.*

Life is full of surprises

Don Kaufman is in a toy store. He is taking a break from delivering mail to buy a toy bear. He doesn't think that anyone is watching him. Then he turns around.

"Oh, you caught me!" Kaufman says. "But this bear isn't for me. It's for . . . Wait, I'm not going to tell you. You have to hear the whole story. It has to do with Ruth and Walter Adams. They found out that life is full of surprises."

Do you think Kaufman is buying the toy bear for himself?

Ruth Adams has a surprise for Walter

Walter Adams is reading the paper. Ruth is trying to talk to him, but he isn't listening.

"You're late?" Walter asks. "Late for what?"

"Oh, come on, Walter," Ruth says. "Put the paper down and listen!"

"When you call me *Walter*, I know I'm in trouble," he says. Ruth usually calls him Walt. "What is it?"

"I think I'm pregnant," says Ruth.

Do you think that Walter will listen to Ruth now?

Walter can't believe it

Ruth's period is 17 days late. All the signs say that she is pregnant. Walter is very surprised. He wonders why Ruth didn't tell him before.

"I wanted to be sure," says Ruth. "I know we really don't want any more kids."

Do you think that Ruth's pregnancy was planned?

It's never too late

Ruth explains about the home pregnancy test she bought at the store. She put a few drops of her urine into the solution. This made a ring. The ring showed that Ruth was pregnant.

Ruth and Walter already have two children. Tyrone is 16 and Pat is 13.

"This is no time to start another family," Walter says. "We're too old."

"Lots of people are having children later now," says Ruth.

Why do you think that more people are having children later now?

Walter worries

It was once a problem to have a baby as you got older. Now it is not such a problem. But Walter has other worries.

"What will this do to Tyrone and Pat? And what about money?" Walter asks.

Ruth had known that Walter would be upset. She wants to wait to see what the doctor will tell her. To Ruth, being pregnant is not the end of the world.

How would you feel if you were Ruth?

Congratulations, Ruth!

Ruth goes to see the doctor. Sure enough, she finds out that she is pregnant. But Ruth doesn't even smile when she hears the news. She says that she is too old to be pregnant.

"You're only 38," says the doctor. "You're fine. You just have to give yourself a little more care."

Ruth has already given herself a test.
Why does she go to see the doctor?

Ruth will gain weight

The doctor begins to tell Ruth about how to take care of herself.

"Your diet probably isn't bad now," says the doctor. "But there are some things that you should do."

"Like don't gain over twenty pounds?" Ruth asks.

"Times have changed," the doctor says.

Now, Ruth can gain up to twenty-five pounds. That will include the weight of the baby.

"Let this baby be light!" says Ruth.

How can the doctor tell that Ruth's diet isn't too bad now?

Doctor's orders

The doctor tells Ruth that she will need more calories now. Ruth is sure she can do that because she likes to eat. But she doesn't like milk. And now she will have to drink a quart of milk a day. Green and yellow vegetables are also on Ruth's diet.

Name some vegetables that are on Ruth's diet.

Ruth's diet won't be easy

Ruth must eat fruit and one serving of whole grain cereal each day. She must eat whole grain bread, too. She must have at least five eggs a week. She should eat fish and lean red meat. She will need all the iron that she can get.

There are some things that Ruth should *not* eat. She must cut out salt, high-fat foods, and most sugar. That part of her diet will be very hard for her.

What do you think of Ruth's diet?

A vitamin a day

The doctor wants Ruth to take some special vitamins, too. Ruth should take one vitamin pill each day. These multivitamins will give Ruth extra milligrams of iron, calcium, and vitamin C. The doctor hopes that the vitamins will help keep Ruth healthy. But Ruth must be sure to follow her diet, too.

Why does Ruth need vitamins along with her new diet?

Rules to live by

Then the doctor says something very important to Ruth.

"TAKE NO OTHER PILLS!" the doctor says. "Don't even take aspirin! And you must not drink any alcohol or smoke, either."

"Being pregnant at my age is hard!" says Ruth.

"These rules having nothing to do with age," says the doctor. "You just have to take care of yourself. You can keep your part-time job. At least for now."

Why is it important for a pregnant woman to take care of herself?

Tyrone thinks that he's in trouble

Ruth and Walter want to tell their children the news about the baby. They will do it that night at dinner.

"I'm full!" says Tyrone after he finishes his dinner. "I don't want to be *too* full. I'm playing B-ball with Clarence tonight."

"Your father has something to tell you," Ruth begins.

"What did you do, Tyrone?" asks Pat.

"Did my French teacher call?" Tyrone asks.

Why does Tyrone ask if his French teacher has called?

Walter breaks the news

Walter begins to talk.

"We're going to have . . ." Walter stops talking and begins again. "*You're* going to have a little brother or sister."

Tyrone doesn't understand yet. But Pat does.

"A baby!" Pat shouts. She is very happy.

Then Tyrone catches on, too.

Why do you think Tyrone doesn't understand at first?

More news is on the way

"A baby?" asks Tyrone. "This is a real surprise!" It was a surprise to Walter, too.

"And now we have to talk about money," says Walter.

"We're lucky," says Ruth. "Your father makes a good living."

"Are we talking about the same man?" asks Tyrone. Tyrone doesn't think that his father makes enough money.

How would you explain a "good living"?

The family budget

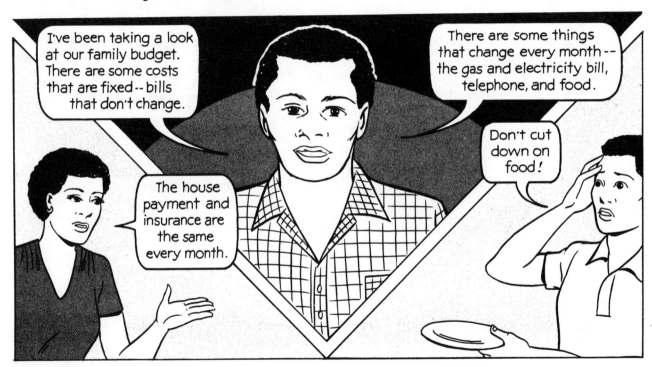

Walter has taken a look at the family budget. The family has two kinds of bills every month: bills that stay the same and bills that change. The house payment and insurance are *fixed* bills.

The bills that change every month are the gas and electricity bill, the telephone bill, and the food bill. The bills that change are the things that the family can cut down on.

What things would be easy for you to cut down on?

The budget doesn't include steak

Walter says that the family can spend less on food. Tyrone thinks that he won't have enough to eat because of the baby.

"That isn't true," says Ruth. "We just can't waste anything."

Pat wants to know what they will name the baby. But they have a long time to decide on that.

"Clear the table before you leave, Mr. Basketball," Ruth says to Tyrone.

Tyrone thinks that Mr. Basketball is a good name for the new baby!

How well did Pat and Tyrone take the news about the baby?

Names have meanings

Kaufman tells us that everyone has thought up a name for the Adams baby. And every name means something.

Suppose someone's name is Smith. Long ago there probably was a blacksmith in the family. Or there may have been a silversmith. Suppose a name ends in "son" or "sky." They both mean "son of." The name "Anderson" means "son of Ander."

If Ruth could pick a name for Walter right now, it would be *Mud*. It sounds as if Ruth is angry at Walter.

How can you tell that Ruth is angry at Walter?

Marge plans a trip

Ruth is buying food at Frank and Marge Marciano's store. Marge is ringing up the cost of the food.

Marge tells Ruth about a store in Carson. The store sells maternity clothes at a discount.

"I'm going to Carson tomorrow," says Marge. "Do you want to come along?"

"Sure, I'll take a look," says Ruth.

But Ruth probably won't buy much. She plans to make some of her own maternity clothes.

Ruth does not plan to buy many clothes in Carson.
Why do you think she wants to go there?

Ruth may take time off

Marge tells Ruth that she will pick her up tomorrow. Together, they will go to Carson. Then Marge asks Ruth if she will quit her job.

"I'll work as long as I can," says Ruth. "I may take sick leave for six weeks after the baby comes. I don't know yet."

"What does Walter want you to do?" Marge asks.

"He really doesn't talk much about the baby," says Ruth. "He seems upset about it."

Why do you think Walter might be upset?

Things were different with Frank

Marge thinks that Walter will change his mind about having the baby. But Ruth isn't so sure. Walter has always been a good husband and father. But Ruth is worried that Walter doesn't want another child.

"Did Frank ever act like this?" Ruth asks.

"Are you kidding?" laughs Marge. "Frank *loves* babies. But two was enough for me. There was only one way that we would have another baby. I told Frank that he would have to carry it himself!"

How can people with different ideas come to an agreement?

Kaufman knows Ruth and Walter's story

Kaufman is writing a book. He meets a lot of people on his job as a mail carrier. They give him ideas for his stories. He says another good story has to do with Ruth and Walter Adams.

Ruth Adams is pregnant. Walter is upset about having a third child. Ruth talks to their friends, Marge and Frank Marciano, about Walter. Frank tries to cheer up Walter, but that doesn't do much good. About that time Ruth and Walter begin taking childbirth classes.

Why do Ruth and Walter go to a childbirth class *together*?

Walter feels out of place

Ruth and Walter are in their childbirth class. Walter is *not* having a good time. He doesn't feel happy about being there. But Ruth's doctor wants them to work together on getting ready for the birth. That is why they have come.

"Look at the other people here," says Walter. "Everyone is young but us."

"*They* don't care how old we are," says Ruth. "But they might wonder why you never smile."

Do you think Walter will learn anything in the childbirth classes?

Learn to relax

The teacher comes into the classroom and starts speaking.

"Childbirth is a natural act," the teacher says. "You want to be ready to take part in it. And you want to be relaxed when you go into delivery. The breathing exercises that you learn here will help you relax. OK, let's get our pillows and get down on the floor. First, we'll do breathing exercises."

What exercises do you do?

The couples learn special breathing

The class practices slow sleep breathing. This kind of breathing helps a woman relax as her contractions get harder. The air goes in fast through the nose. Then it goes out slowly through the mouth.

Besides slow breathing, what else might help a woman relax?

What's good about the goodie bag?

Every couple has to take a goodie bag with them to the hospital. In it are lollipops for the woman, a cool washcloth to wipe her face, and warm socks for her feet. A sock with tennis balls is used for back labor. And the men will get the cookies. They might be hungry.

"Now let's do the pant-blow breathing exercise," the teacher says. "Use this when you want to push, but the doctor says not to."

Why do you think the goodie bag might be a good idea?

It's Walter and Ruth's turn

The couples are all making loud breathing noises. Walter thinks that the breathing sounds funny. He helps Ruth do her exercise. But he does not enjoy doing it.

"Everyone can stop now," the teacher says. "Walter and Ruth, will you help me? Let's show the class the next exercise."

Walter makes a face.

"Oh, boy!" says Ruth. "This is going to be a long night."

Does Ruth really feel that Walter is a big help?

Tyrone eats like a horse

It is dinner time at the Adamses' house. Tyrone eats a lot. He is a growing boy and he is healthy. Today he and Rick Esteban ran against two other boys. They ran five track races and won all of them.

"You and Mom are in great shape, too, Dad," Tyrone says. "Not like Mr. Marciano. When I work at the store, he eats things behind his wife's back. He asks me to watch out for Mrs. Marciano. But I let her catch him eating the other day."

Why do you think Tyrone let Marge catch Frank eating?

A car pool saves gas

"Speaking of jobs and money," says Ruth, "I think that our new money plan is working."

The family is saving some money. Walter has joined a car pool. That has really cut down on gas. In fact, 40% of the money that they saved last month was on gas.

Would you join a car pool to get to work?

Where the money goes

I learned in class how families spend their take-home pay. 25% to 30% goes for housing. 19% to 22% goes for food.

Transportation takes about 14% to 16%. Clothes take 9%.

Everything else is 25% to 30%.

That's about right for us. Our "everything else" may be less and our "food" more, thanks to Tyrone.

Thanks a lot.

Pat shows the family a list that she made in family life class. The list shows how a family spends its take-home pay: 25% to 30% for housing, 19% to 22% for food, 14% to 16% for transportation, 9% for clothes, and 25% to 30% for everything else.

Ruth says that their family spends less on "everything else." But they spend *more* on food.

Do you think that Pat's list is true for *your* family?

Ruth tells how they saved money

Ruth tells the family how they saved money. First, the gas and electricity bill was smaller. And Ruth bought some things at discount stores. Discount stores often charge less than other stores.

Ruth also paid off two credit card bills. When people don't pay in full, the credit card company charges interest. Ruth saved money by paying the charges off on time. From now on, the family will be careful about using credit cards.

How can you cut down on gas and electricity?

Pat and Tyrone surprise their father

Pat has something on her mind.

"Is there something wrong about the baby?" Pat asks Walter. "You don't act happy about it."

Walter looks surprised. Pat has guessed that he is upset about having a third child.

"What do you mean?" Walter asks.

"Is there something we should know?" Tyrone asks. He, too, thinks that something is wrong.

How can Pat tell that Walter is upset?

Walter faces the facts

Walter is worried about raising another child. He doesn't want the kids to know that. But Pat wants to talk about the baby.

"We're old enough to talk about it," Pat says. "This is *your* baby. But all four of us will be its family."

"Ruth, let's have a talk," says Walter.

Why does Walter want to talk to Ruth?

Ruth is doing fine

Ruth is in the doctor's office talking about Walter. She says he is feeling better about the baby. He is finally coming around to the idea.

Ruth's weight is just right. She has cut out both salt and sugar. She is eating only what the doctor has told her to eat. After all, the baby gets everything that Ruth eats.

Why is it so important for Ruth to eat well?

Easy does it

Ruth tells the doctor that the kids are happy about the baby. Tyrone is even painting the extra room the baby will use.

"It's good to do it now," the doctor says. "The paint smell would be bad for the baby."

Then the doctor checks Ruth's blood pressure. It is a little high. High blood pressure could hurt the baby. So Ruth will need a checkup every week from now on.

Why does the doctor want to check Ruth every week?

The star player

The doctor tells Ruth to get eight hours of sleep every night. Ruth should take a walk every day, too. Exercise will help Ruth sleep better.

"Who can sleep?" Ruth laughs. "This baby kicks all night!"

"That's OK," says the doctor. "They say that soccer is the wave of the future."

Ruth knows that the baby is strong.

"I must be carrying the star of the team!" Ruth says.

What do parents often wish for their child's future?

Kaufman enjoys Ruth's company

Kaufman brings us up to date on Ruth.

Ruth is now in her eighth month of pregnancy. She is working only three days a week. And sometimes she walks along with Kaufman while he delivers mail. Kaufman enjoys talking to her.

Everything is going fine with Ruth. Then one night Ruth, Walter, Frank, and Marge go out to dinner.

What might Kaufman and Ruth talk about on their walks?

Frank can't stop eating

Ruth, Walter, Frank, and Marge are in a restaurant. They are just finishing dinner. Frank says that he is so full he can't eat another bite.

"No wonder, Frank," says Marge. "You ate your meal and most of mine. I'd be full, too!"

Frank looks at Ruth's dish. She still has some food left. Now Frank wants to eat that, too!

Would you like to go out to dinner with Frank?

Table talk

Ruth tells the others about her last trip to the doctor. She found out that the baby has turned already. It won't be long now! Ruth and Walter have not picked a name yet.

"I like Ike!" Frank jokes. "Or a good Italian name such as Saverio."

"Italian names won't work for us, Frank," says Walter.

Do you like the name your parents gave you?

The time has come

Suddenly, Ruth lets out a scream.

"What's wrong, Ruth?" Walter asks. "Did the baby kick you again?"

Ruth knows it wasn't a kick. It felt more like a contraction. But the baby isn't due for another month. Ruth seems to be going into labor. She wants to leave the restaurant.

Frank is more excited than Ruth. Marge has to tell him to be quiet.

Why does Frank keep shouting, "Oh, my stomach!"?

Frank makes a scene

Frank shouts at the waitress for the check. He is very excited.

"Frank, calm down!" says Marge. "Walter, how far are we from the hospital?"

Walter doesn't know. He only knows how to get to the hospital from his home. Then the waitress comes over to ask if something is wrong. Marge tells her Ruth is in labor.

How do you think the waitress might help?

Marge is in the driver's seat

Marge asks the waitress how far away the hospital is.

"About three miles," answers the waitress. It will take them from five to fifteen minutes to drive to the hospital.

Marge thinks that Frank is too excited to drive. So Marge will drive to the hospital herself.

"You help Walter with Ruth," Marge tells Frank.

Ruth wants to leave right away. Her contractions are coming closer together. The baby is on its way.

Who is helping Ruth the most? How is that person helping?

Things are happening fast

Things are happening too fast for Walter. He and Ruth are in the delivery room already. Walter doesn't even have the goodie bag with him. And Ruth is afraid that something is wrong. The baby is coming too early. It is too late for the slow sleep breathing exercise. She tries the pant-blow exercise. Walter helps her.

A nurse tells them that the doctor is getting ready.

"Don't worry," the nurse says. "Everything is fine."

Why does Ruth do her breathing exercises?

The doctor takes over

Walter helps Ruth do the pant-blow breathing exercise. He is very excited.

"This is it!" Walter says.

"It seems to be," the doctor says. She is very calm. "Now, just relax."

Ruth wants to know if everything is OK.

"All your signs are fine," the doctor says. "Maybe this baby just can't wait to get here."

How can you tell that Ruth's doctor is a good one?

A baby is born

At last the baby is born. It is the first time Walter has seen his wife give birth. It is beautiful.

"It's here!" Walter shouts. "I can see it!"

"You can say 'her,'" says the doctor. "She's a beautiful little girl!"

Do you think Ruth is glad that Walter is with her?

Tell the world

"Oh, look, Walter!" cries Ruth. "Is she OK?"

"She looks fine to me," the doctor answers.

Ruth wants Walter to tell Frank and Marge about their baby girl.

"And tell the kids, too," says Ruth. "I want them to see her right away!"

Do you think Walter is still upset about having a third child?

Elizabeth says hello

The doctor brings the baby to Ruth.

"Do you want to hold her?" the doctor asks.

"Oh, yes!" says Ruth.

The doctor hands Ruth the little baby girl. Ruth holds her in her arms. She looks at her little face. The baby is crying, but she is very healthy. Ruth smiles and says, "Welcome home, Elizabeth!"

When do you think Ruth picked the name "Elizabeth"?